## *Book brief*

1. Meghan is just an ordinary teenager from the north of England but one day, her parents give her some bad news.

2. Meghan and her family have got big problems and they need help.

3. Meghan has got other problems too but she can't tell anyone.

4. Then, Meghan makes an unexpected friend and things start to change for the better.

5. Main themes include family, friendship, food waste, poverty and online bullying.



www.eligradedreaders.

## *In this reader:*

| | |
|---|---|
| 21st Century Skills | To encourage students to connect the story to the world they live in. |
| Key | A2 level activities. |
| Simple Story | A brief summary of the paragraph. |
| Glossary | Explanation of difficult words. |
| Picture Caption | A brief explanation of the picture. |
| Audio | These icons indicate the parts of the story that are recorded. start / stop |
| Think | To encourage students to develop their critical thinking skills. |

*Sarah Gudgeon*

# The Yellow Sticker Girl

*Illustrated by*
**Luca Tagliafico**

Teen ELi Readers

## Teen Eli Readers

The **ELI Readers** collection is a complete range of books and plays for readers of all ages, ranging from captivating contemporary stories to timeless classics. There are four series, each catering for a different age group: **First ELI Readers, Young ELI Readers, Teen ELI Readers** and **Young Adult ELI Readers**. The books are carefully edited and beautifully illustrated to capture the essence of the stories and plots. The readers are supplemented with 'Focus on' texts packed with background cultural information about the writers and their lives and times.


*The Yellow Sticker Girl*
*by* **Sarah Gudgeon**

*Illustrated by* **Luca Tagliafico**

**ELI Readers**
*Founder and Series Editors*
**Paola Accattoli, Grazia Ancillani, Daniele Garbuglia (Art Director)**

*Graphic Design*
**Emilia Coari**

*Production Manager*
**Francesco Capitano**

*Photo credits*
**Shutterstock**

*First edition:* **2023**





**P.O. Box 6**
**62019 Recanati MC**
**Italy**
**T +39 071750701**
**F +39 071977851**
**info@elionline.com**
**www.elionline.com**



*Typeset in 12 / 17 pt*
**Fulmar designed by Leo Philp**

*Printed in Italy by*
**Tecnostampa - Pigini Group Printing Division**
**Loreto - Trevi - ERT278.10**
**ISBN 978-88-536-3962-2**

**www.eligradedreaders.com**

## *Contents*

Meghan
Dad
Mr Turner

Kyla
Mum
Leah

## Before you read

### **Reading** · A2 Key

**1 Complete the text about the book with the correct answer (A, B or C).**

Meghan lives with her mum, dad and younger sister Leah in __the__ north of England. They are a happy family but one day Meghan's dad (**1**) ______ some bad news. Life becomes more difficult and they don't have (**2**) ______ money for food and bills. Meghan and her parents do everything they (**3**) ______ to survive the crisis and to protect Leah from the reality of their situation. Meghan doesn't (**4**) ______ her parents but she's got another problem too: Kyla. (**5**) ______ is she so mean to Meghan and why do the other kids listen to her? Meghan hates going (**6**) ______ school.

| | | | |
|---|---|---|---|
| | **A** up | ~~**B**~~ the | **C** east |
| **1** | **A** receives | **B** listens | **C** finds |
| **2** | **A** too | **B** many | **C** enough |
| **3** | **A** can | **B** might | **C** need |
| **4** | **A** say | **B** tell | **C** speak |
| **5** | **A** What | **B** When | **C** Why |
| **6** | **A** at | **B** to | **C** for |

### **Speaking** 21st Century Skills

**2 At the start of the story Meghan is hungry and wants a snack. Discuss these questions about food and eating habits with a partner.**

1. How many meals a day do you have?
2. What do you usually have for breakfast / lunch / dinner?
3. What's your favourite food?
4. How important is it for people to eat healthily?
5. Is junk food more or less expensive than fresh food in your country?
6. Who does most of the cooking in your house?

## Listening · A2 Key

2 **3 Listen to the start of chapter 1 and write one word in each gap.**

Meghan and her family always had fish and chips on *Friday* nights.

1 They had ______ on Saturday nights.
2 Meghan's favourite ______ were vanilla yoghurt, strawberries and chocolate biscuits.
3 Meghan opened the fridge one day in ______ and it was empty.
4 Meghan wanted some ______ .
5 Meghan's mum and ______ came into the kitchen.
6 Meghan's parents need to talk to her about ______ .

## Writing

21st Century Skills

**4 Answer these questions.**

1 What do you usually do on Friday and Saturday nights?
2 Do you usually eat the same food? Why? / Why not?
3 Do you prefer eating at home or in a restaurant? Why? / Why not?
4 Do you prefer to eat with friends or family?
5 Do you prefer sweet or savoury snacks?
6 What are your favourite snacks?

__________________________________________
__________________________________________
__________________________________________
__________________________________________
__________________________________________
__________________________________________
__________________________________________
__________________________________________
__________________________________________
__________________________________________

### Chapter 1

# That Nickname

2 I never really thought about food until last spring. My mum always made nice things like spag bol[1] or sausage and beans for our tea[2]. On Friday nights we always had fish and chips, Saturdays were for pizza and on Sundays we had a big roast dinner. When I was hungry in the afternoons, I just went to the kitchen and got something from the fridge. Mum always bought my favourite snacks like vanilla yoghurt, strawberries and chocolate biscuits. But one day after school, in March, I opened the fridge and ... it was empty.

'Mum,' I shouted up the stairs. 'There's no food in the fridge and I'm starving[3]!' Of course, I wasn't really starving, we had school meals at lunchtime, but I did want some chocolate.

Meghan is very hungry but there is no food in the fridge. Mum and dad want to talk to her. Meghan is very worried.

Anyway, mum came down the stairs and into the kitchen, followed by dad. *Now that was weird. Why wasn't dad at work?*

'Meghan, me and dad need to talk to you about something,' mum said. *Uh oh, this was serious.*

1 **spag bol** spaghetti with bolognese sauce
2 **tea** the name for 'dinner' in the north of England
3 **starving** very hungry

*Mum only ever called me Meghan when I was in trouble*[1].

'It's OK, Meggie. Don't look so worried,' Dad added.

3 Ok, so maybe no-one was dead and they weren't getting divorced. Phew!

Maybe it was about that maths test I did last week then. My teacher, Mrs Bright, said she was a bit disappointed[2] with my result... No, wait a minute, maybe our neighbour Mr Cullen was angry because I went over his flowers on my bike ... but that was just an accident.

'Meggie? Are you listening to me? I said we're just having a bit of money trouble, that's all,' dad tried to reassure me.

'What kind of money trouble?' I asked. 'Mum's working full-time and you have some hours at the biscuit factory.'

'I know, Meggie, but since I lost my job things have been hard,' dad explained.

'And today the factory bosses told dad they don't have any work for him,' mum continued.

*OMG! We're going to be poor!*

'Does this mean that we're going to lose our

**Meghan doesn't know what her parents want to talk to her about. They tell her that they haven't got a lot of money. Meghan's dad has lost his job.**

1 **was in trouble** did something wrong
2 **disappointed** sad

house and have no money for food or clothes?' I asked, suddenly feeling very scared.

The family must spend their money carefully.

'Of course not,' mum and dad replied in unison but they didn't look very convinced[1].

'It just means that we'll have to be more careful with our money,' mum said.

Hmmm ... that didn't sound too bad but I was about to discover that it was in fact very bad.

I left mum and dad drinking a cup of tea around the kitchen table - tea is the solution to everything in our house - and went to the garden. Leah was sitting on the grass talking to her teddies. Leah is my little sister. She's totally cute and everyone loves her. Leah was organising a tea party with her bear friends - I told you tea is a big thing for us - and invited me to join them.

'Meg, come and have some tea and cake,' she said.

Meghan goes to play in the garden with her little sister, Leah. They are hungry and want a snack.

'Thank you very much, Miss Leah,' I replied as I tried to find a space between all the other guests.

Leah served the imaginary tea and cake but after about an hour of this game, we were both a bit peckish[2].

'I'll go and get us a real snack now, Leah,'

›

Mum, dad and Meghan talk about their money problems.

1 **convinced** sure
2 **peckish** a little hungry

I offered. Maybe mum would give me some money for ice cream. *We had enough money for ice cream, right?*

'Mum! Can I have some money for an ice cream for me and Leah, please?' I shouted as I walked into the kitchen.

Mum and dad were still sitting at the table and their sad faces answered my question.

There isn't any money for an ice cream. They have to go to the supermarket after 6:00 p.m.

'Sorry, love,' dad offered, 'we'll go to the supermarket later and get something after 6p.m.'

*After 6p.m? Totally weird! We normally had our tea at 6p.m.*

'Can we go now, dad?' I asked but dad just shook his head and told me to go out and play with Leah again. Oh no, Leah. She's waiting for her ice cream. *I need an idea ... Got it!*

Meghan and her sister Leah have an imaginary snack.

'Hey, Leah,' I shouted. 'I've got an amazing[1] magic ice-cream sundae for you.'

'Where is it?' she asked, really excited.

'It's magic, remember. You can't see it but you can taste it,' I told her. 'Mine is raspberry, strawberry and vanilla. Delicious[2]! What does yours taste like?'

Leah stuck out her tongue and closed her eyes in concentration.

1 **amazing** brilliant
2 **delicious** very nice

## The Yellow Sticker Girl

'Hmm ... mine tastes like chocolate bubbles, apple pie and blueberry muffins,' Leah squealed[1] with delight.

'Wow! That sounds SO good, Leah,' I replied as we both laughed and ate our pretend sundaes.

We were just about to have magic milkshakes when dad called me.

'Come on Meggie, let's go and do the shopping. We can take the 17:40 bus and be there just in time.'

Just in time? Just in time for what, I wondered. I didn't have to wait long to find out.

Dad and I arrived at the supermarket at 18:02. He didn't stop at the newspaper stand on the way in or take a look at the cakes and doughnuts. Now, that was strange; this was a man who never walked past baked goods without an appreciative sniff[2]. He just grabbed[3] a shopping trolley and ran into the store. He went straight to the chiller cabinets in aisle[4] 17. Actually, he went to one specific shelf. There were all different kinds of food on this shelf from chicken to hummus to quiche but they all had the same yellow sticker. There was a man putting the stickers on while dad looked.

**Meghan and her dad take the bus to the supermarket.**

**Meghan's dad goes straight to the shelf where there is food with a yellow sticker on it. This food costs less after 6p.m.**

1 **squealed** made a loud sound of excitement
2 **sniff** smell
3 **grabbed** quickly took
4 **aisle** a passage between supermarket shelves

'Come over here, Meggie,' he shouted. 'Let's choose something for tea tonight. They reduce the price of everything after 6p.m.'

Meghan's dad is happy because he finds food for their tea.

Dad was happily putting food in our trolley when suddenly I heard someone laughing. I turned round and saw Kyla Jackson from my year at school. *Oh no! What does SHE want?* Kyla is the class bully and she can make your life a nightmare[1]. She was with a couple of other girls and they were all laughing and pointing at me.

Meghan is embarrassed because Kyla and some other girls see her and take photos.

*Great! What are they doing now?!* Kyla had her mobile phone and was taking pictures of me. *No! Photos! Why did she want photos of me at the supermarket with my dad?!* I was so embarrassed I just wanted to disappear.

'Come on, dad. Let's go,' I whispered[2].

'Ok, Meggie-Moo. Maybe we can get some ice cream too,' he said and walked off to the frozen food aisle, past Kyla and her gang[3].

I followed him, head down, and as I walked past, Kyla said in a sing-song voice 'Bye, yellow sticker girl!' *What?!*

1 **nightmare** a bad dream
2 **whispered** spoke quietly
3 **gang** a group

Kyla takes a photo of Meghan at the supermarket.

## Reading Comprehension

**1 Read the questions about Chapter 1. Tick answer A or B.**

What did Meghan do when she was hungry in the afternoons?
~~A~~ She went to the fridge. **B** She went to the supermarket.

**1** What happened one day in March?
**A** There were extra snacks in the fridge.
**B** There were no snacks in the fridge.

**2** Why do Meghan and her family have to be careful with money?
**A** Because there is no work for her dad.
**B** Because her mum doesn't work.

**3** What time do Meghan and her dad go to the supermarket?
**A** After 6:00 a.m. **B** After 6:00 p.m.

**4** How do they get to the supermarket?
**A** On foot. **B** By bus.

**5** What was on the food that Meghan's dad was looking at?
**A** Yellow stickers. **B** Red dots.

**6** Who is Kyla?
**A** The class repesentative. **B** The class bully.

## Grammar

**2 Complete the sentences in the past simple. Use the verbs in brackets.**

Meghan *went* (go) to the fridge but it was empty.

**1** Her parents ________ (come) downstairs to talk to her.
**2** Meghan ________ (play) with Leah in the garden.
**3** Meghan and Leah ________ (be) hungry.
**4** Meghan and her dad ________ (get) the bus to the supermarket.
**5** Meghan's dad ________ (walk) directly to aisle 17.
**6** Meghan ________ (see) Kyla and some other girls laughing and taking a photo of her.

## Speaking

21st Century Skills

**3** **Look again at the picture of Kyla and the other girls laughing at Meghan. They have posted her photo on social media. Discuss these questions with a partner.**

1 What do you take photos of on your phone or another device?

2 Do you use social media? Why/ Why not?

3 Do you post selfies? Why / Why not?

4 Do you share photos of your friends online? Why / Why not?

5 Is it OK to post photos of other people without their permission?

6 Do you ever feel embarrassed about your online photos?

***Before-reading Activity***

## Listening

4 **4** **Listen to the start of Chapter 2 and decide if the sentences are true (T) or false (F).**

| | | T | F |
|---|---|---|---|
| | Meghan's new nickname is The Yellow Sticker Girl. | ☑ | ☐ |
| 1 | Meghan thinks it is a beautiful nickname. | ☐ | ☐ |
| 2 | Kyla posted Meghan's photo on social media. | ☐ | ☐ |
| 3 | Some people wrote nice comments. | ☐ | ☐ |
| 4 | No one laughed at Meghan at school. | ☐ | ☐ |
| 5 | Kyla was Meghan's best friend at primary school. | ☐ | ☐ |
| 6 | Meghan saw a sign in a bakery window. | ☐ | ☐ |

## Chapter 2

# Happy Saturdays

The kids at school call Meghan The Yellow Sticker Girl. They write horrible things about her on social media.

4 The Yellow Sticker Girl. That was my new nickname[1] at school. It wasn't a nice nickname like 'Meggie' or 'Meg' or even 'Meggie-Moo' (which was quite embarrassing at my age!), it was horrible. Kyla posted my photo at the supermarket all over social media with the hashtag #theyellowstickergirl. All my classmates saw the photo and some people even left nasty[2] comments like 'They're a family of tramps[3],' and 'They look in rubbish bins for their tea as well.' *What is wrong with these people? Don't they know that just because we haven't got a lot of money at the moment, we're still just a normal family?* Other kids at school laughed at me when I walked down the corridor and no one wanted to sit next to me at lunchtime. *Thanks, Kyla!* I can't believe she was my best friend at primary school.

Meghan is very unhappy at school. She sees a sign in the bakery window.

Anyway, school was a nightmare and I couldn't wait for the bell to ring at the end of every day and go home. One day, I was walking home on my own when I saw a sign in the bakery window.

1 **nickname** an invented name, connected to a person's character or appearance

2 **nasty** horrible

3 **tramps** people who have no home or job and ask for food or money in the street

# The Yellow Sticker Girl

5 It was for a 'Saturday Girl'. *Hmmm ... a part time job?* I looked in through the bakery window. There were a couple of ladies standing behind the counter[1], putting bread and cakes into paper bags. *Cake! Yum!* There was carrot cake, egg custards, iced fingers and lots more too! The shop was full of customers in a long queue[2], but everyone was smiling and waiting patiently. I decided to be brave[3] and go in. As soon as I opened the door I was hit by the amazing smell of freshly baked[4] bread. *I have to work here!* Suddenly, a loud voice shouted out from round the back.

**Meghan sees a job advertisement at a bakery. The job is only on Saturdays and Meghan decides to be brave and ask the owner.**

'The muffins are out of the oven. Get your muffins!'

And then, the owner of the voice appeared. Mr Turner was a large, round man (I suppose that's what happens when you eat delicious cakes every day) with an equally round smiley face. *Ok, Meghan, you can do it. Ask him about the job.*

'Excuse me, Sir,' I shouted. 'I saw the ad[5] in the window for a Saturday girl.'

'Ah yes,' replied Mr Turner as he came to the front of the counter.

1 **counter** where the shop assistant puts the things you buy
2 **queue** a line of people
3 **brave** courageous
4 **freshly baked** just out of the oven
5 **ad** advertisement

'Do you have any experience?' he asked.

'Erm ... no ... but I LOVE cake,' I replied hopefully.

Mr Turner laughed.

'Well, I suppose that is the main requirement[1] for someone who wants to work in a bakery,' he said. 'Can you start next week?'

'Yes!!! Sorry, I mean yes, please. Thank you,' I laughed nervously.

There was one thing I had to tell Mr Turner though before I left.

'Mr Turner?'

'Yes, dear,' he answered.

Meghan hasn't worked in a bakery before but she loves cake. Mr Turner gives Meghan the job. She is very happy but tells him to advertise for a Saturday Person. Mr Turner also gives Meghan some free cake.

'Do you know that you can't advertise for a Saturday Girl? We're in the 21st century now, you have to advertise for a Saturday Person. I'm sure there are boys who like cake too,' I laughed.

'You're absolutely right, dear,' replied Mr Turner. He went to the shop window, took the sign down, crossed out[2] 'girl' and wrote 'person'.

'I need another Saturday PERSON,' he said. 'This is a very busy[3] bakery'.

Mr Turner gave me my uniform, some FREE CAKE (Leah is going to love my new job!) and

›

1 **requirement** something you need
2 **crossed out** drew a line through
3 **busy** full of work and activity

Meghan sees an ad for a Saturday Girl.

SATURDAY GIRL WANTED
APPLY WITHIN

I went home feeling super-happy! Finally, there was some good news!

6 On the Saturday morning I was really nervous. I went downstairs for breakfast and there was a surprise waiting for me: a full English breakfast[1]. Dad was putting everything onto a big plate.

Meghan's dad makes her and Leah a big breakfast before her first day at work. Meghan is sad because there isn't enough food for her parents.

'You're a worker now,' he said. 'You need a good breakfast.'

'Thanks, dad,' I smiled back.

Leah came into the kitchen then with mum. There was bacon and eggs for her too but mum and dad just had a cup of tea.

'Where's your breakfast?' I asked but they just shook their heads and said, 'We're not hungry this morning, love. Eat up[2]!'

Leah is too young to understand and happily ate her breakfast but I was already thinking about the first thing I wanted to buy with my wages[3]: bacon and eggs for everyone!

After breakfast, I went upstairs and got my uniform on. The red skirt and red and white striped blouse made me feel very important - *I have a real job!* - but I wasn't too sure about

1 **a full English breakfast** sausage, bacon, eggs, beans and tomatoes
2 **eat up** finish your food
3 **wages** the money your boss pays you every week

the white hat. Mum, dad and Leah all thought I looked great of course.

'You look beautiful,' said mum.

'Yes, and so professional too,' added dad.

'CUTE!!!!' laughed Leah.

Everyone agrees that she looks very nice in her uniform.

I walked to the bus stop feeling happy and confident. The 204 bus came on time and ten minutes later I was in town. I had butterflies in my tummy[1] but I was excited too. While I was walking to the bakery I saw Kyla and some of the other girls but luckily they didn't see me. I decided to go straight to the bakery. A run in[2] with Kyla before my new job? No thanks! I was a few minutes early but Mr Turner was just happy to see me.

Meghan sees Kyla and some girls when she is walking to work but they don't see her.

'Come on in, Kyla dear,' he welcomed me. 'We're busy this morning. Get your hat on!'

I spent the next four hours serving bread and cake, smiling at customers and trying to resist the temptation to eat a strawberry tart! Everyone was so nice and the morning passed really quickly. At the end of my shift[3] Mr Turner came to talk to me.

1 **butterflies in my tummy** feel nervous
2 **run in** confrontation
3 **shift** the numbers of hours you work in one day

**Mr Turner is very happy with Meghan. He gives her her money plus bread and cakes.**

'Well done, Meghan,' he complimented me. 'You worked really hard, you're smart and the customers love you.'

'Wow, thanks Mr Turner,' I replied.

Then he gave me an envelope with my wages in and a bag of bread and cakes.

'We don't like to waste[1] food,' he said.

I love my job!

**Meghan loves her job and uses her money for gifts and her mobile phone.**

I went to the bakery every week. Saturday was my favourite day of the week. There was even a new Saturday Boy 😉. I used my wages to buy treats[2] for all the family. I didn't need to ask mum and dad to top up[3] my mobile phone anymore either, I used my money. Saturdays were my escape from the nightmare of school until, one day, I saw Kyla and some other girls at the bus stop. I was waiting for the bus to go to work when I heard 'Hey! Yellow Sticker Girl!' *Oh no! Not here as well!* I looked over the road and Kyla was taking another photo of me … in my uniform.

**One day Kyla and some girls take photos of Meghan in her uniform.**

'Nice clothes,' she shouted.

'Yeah, so trendy,' added one of the other girls laughing.

*Great! What will the next hashtag be?!*

***Think***

**Many students in the UK have a Saturday job. Why do you think young people want to work?**

›

**Kyla takes a photo of Meghan in her uniform**

1 **waste** use inefficiently or throw away
2 **treats** small gifts
3 **top up** buy credit for

## **Reading** · A2 Key

**1 Complete the text about Chapter 2. Write one word in each space.**

Meghan entered the bakery ___*to*___ ask about the Saturday job. Mr Turner offered her (**1**) ________ job and gave her a uniform and (**2**) ________ free cake. Meghan started the following week and she loved (**3**) ________ in the shop. Saturday was her favourite day (**4**) ________ the week. She always (**5**) ________ the bus to work and one day she saw Kyla and some other girls while she was waiting (**6**) ________ the bus stop.

## **Writing**

**2 Underline the correct word in each sentence.**

The other kids at school laughed at Meghan *when* / *while* they saw her.

1 Meghan was walking home from school when she *was seeing* / *saw* a sign in the bakery window.

2 Dad made breakfast for Meghan *when* / *while* she was getting ready for work.

3 Meghan saw Kyla and some other girls while she *was walking* / *walked* to the bakery.

4 Meghan *was loving* / *loved* her new job.

5 One day Meghan was waiting for the bus *when*/ *while* she heard Kyla shout.

6 The other girls *was* / *were* laughing while Kyla was taking the photo.

## Speaking

21st Century Skills

**3 Meghan is embarrassed because she is wearing a uniform. Discuss these questions with a partner.**

1 Do you ever wear a uniform? If yes, what for?
2 Can you name 4 jobs that require workers to wear a uniform?
3 Do you think school uniforms are a good idea? Why / Why not?
4 Do you think uniforms should be the same for boys and girls?
5 Are the clothes you wear an important part of your identity?
6 What is your personal style?

*Before-reading Activity*

## Listening

7 **4 Listen to the start of Chapter 3 and match the sentence halves.**

[e] Meghan didn't turn her phone
1 [ ] On Monday morning her phone
2 [ ] A girl from Meghan's science class
3 [ ] There was a big photo of Meghan
4 [ ] All the other kids were laughing
5 [ ] Meghan ran down the corridor
6 [ ] She locked the cubicle door

a tagged her in one of the posts.
b in her uniform.
c and into the girls toilets.
d and pointing at Meghan.
~~e~~ on all weekend.
f and cried.
g started pinging immediately.

## Chapter 3

# A Bank with a Difference

7 I didn't turn my phone on all weekend, social media was my new enemy, but on Monday morning I had to check my online diary. My phone started pinging[1] immediately. A girl from my science class, who I thought was my friend, tagged me[2] in one of the posts. There was a big photo of me in my uniform and the hashtag this time was #theyellowsticker#fashiondisaster. Ok, so it was embarrassing but luckily I wasn't wearing my hat! Maybe the other kids at school won't even see the photo. Or maybe they will ... as I looked at my screen, comments started to appear: 'No food, no clothes, no life!', 'Total loser![3]'. I heard other phones pinging and that's when the laughing and the pointing started AGAIN! The other kids were all looking at me and I wanted to disappear. *Please, please make me invisible!* There was only one solution: the toilets. I ran down the corridor, into the girls toilets, into a cubicle, locked the door ... and cried. *Why is my life such*

**There is another photo of Meghan on social media. Everyone at school laughs at her and writes horrible comments. Meghan hides in the toilets.**

1 **pinging** the noise a mobile phone makes when a notification arrives

2 **tagged me** put my social media name on a post/ photo

3 **loser** pathetic person

*a nightmare?!* I hated school. I hated Kyla and the other bullies. I just wanted to go home.

8 Home. I know it's a cliché[1] but home really is where the heart is. We didn't have a lot of money but we had a lot of love. Leah was always so happy to see me ... especially when I had cake!

Meghan loves her home and her family. It was a terrible week at school but Leah gives Meghan a painting and she feels better.

'Meggie, Meggie, come and look at my unicorn,' she shouted as I walked through the front door that Saturday after work.

'Hey, Leah! Wow, that's a fabulous unicorn!' I replied as I looked at her latest painting.

'It's for you, Meggie!' she smiled.

'Thank you so much,' I laughed, picking her up for a hug.

I couldn't really see a unicorn among the blue, pink and yellow splodges[2] of paint to be honest, but Leah made it just for me and I felt better already after my terrible week at school.

The other kids were still making fun of me and I didn't want to tell mum and dad because they had enough problems.

'Where are mum and dad?' I asked Leah as I gave her an iced finger.

'In the kitchen. Talking,' she said. 'Grown-up stuff'.

1 **cliché** an unoriginal opinion
2 **splodges** unidentifiable shapes

*Grown up stuff? Uh-oh. Sounds like more trouble.*

'Mum! Dad! I'm home,' I shouted through to the kitchen.

'Just a minute, Meggie. We're coming,' mum shouted back.

I had a feeling that my bad week was about to get worse ... and I was right.

Mum and dad came into the living room, said hello, and then continued whispering in the corner. Dad was holding a couple of pound coins in his hand and mum had something in her hand too. It looked like a letter. *What was it? Who was it from?*

Leah and I were watching some cartoons while she ate her iced finger but after a few minutes mum and dad told me to follow them into the kitchen.

'Come in here in a minute, Meggie. We want to talk to you,' mum said.

Meghan's mum and dad want to speak to her in private. They have got to pay a bill and they have no money for food.

*No more bad news! Please!*

'Ok, Meggie, so the situation is quite bad now,' mum explained. 'We have this gas bill[1] to pay and we have no money for food.'

*No money for food! We really are going to starve!*

Mum and dad haven't got enough money for the gas bill and food.

'Are we going to die, cold and hungry?' I asked my mum in a panic.

1 **bill** money you pay for services like gas and electricity

GAS COMP
FINAL
WARNIN

'We're NOT going to die, Meggie,' mum reassured me, 'but we do need help.'

*My grandparents were dead and mum and dad didn't have any brothers or sisters. Who will help us?*

'There is a food bank[1] in town,' mum continued. 'We can go there for some food today.'

*A food bank? I thought banks were places for people to keep their money...*

'What's a food bank?' I asked.

'It's a charity[2],' dad explained. 'They give people food when they don't have enough money to buy it for themselves.'

*Charity?! Oh no! First the yellow stickers, now free food like homeless people!*

Meghan and her family have to go to a food bank. Meghan is very angry at first and cries. Then, she offers to go to the food bank with her mum. She wants to protect Leah from the situation.

'I don't want charity,' I shouted angrily. 'I don't want to be poor!'

'I know, Meggie,' dad said as he hugged me. 'I know it's a horrible situation but we're lucky that there are organisations that want to help us.'

Even as I cried, I knew that dad was right. I didn't want Leah to be hungry and I didn't want her to know how bad our situation was.

'I'll go with mum,' I offered. 'You stay here and play with Leah, dad'.

1 **food bank** an organisation that gives food to people who cannot pay
2 **charity** a non-profit organisation that helps people

Dad smiled and gave me an even bigger hug.

'My sweet, sweet Meggie,' he said. 'Thank you, love.'

The bus stopped right outside the community food bank on Market Street. Mum and I were both a bit nervous but we were greeted at the door by a volunteer[1].

Meghan and her mum are nervous at the food bank but a woman called Maureen helps them.

'Hi. Come in, come in,' she said. 'My name's Maureen. Is this your first time?'

'Yes, it is,' mum answered hesitantly. 'I'm Abbie and this is my daughter Meghan.'

'Ok. Well, don't worry about anything Abbie and Meghan. I'll show you what to do,' Maureen reassured us.

We walked into a big hall and there was food EVERYWHERE. It was so organised. Maureen gave us a shopping bag and took us to the different tables. On one table there were boxes of pasta, rice and cereal; on another there were tins of soup, tuna, beans and spaghetti hoops and on another there was soap and shampoo.

*Wow! Where did all this stuff come from?!*

'Just choose all the things you need,' said Maureen to mum, 'and I'll go and get you a cup of tea and a biscuit.'

1 **volunteer** a person who gives their time and services for free

Meghan and her mum get their shopping. Maureen makes Meghan's mum feel better.

Mum and I soon had a full bag of shopping. There was even a big fridge in the corner and I found some vanilla yoghurt for me and some chocolate milk for Leah! Before we left, Mum and Maureen had a quick chat[1] about our situation.

'Any family can have problems sometimes,' Maureen reassured mum. 'Just remember, you're not alone. You're part of a community and we're here to help.'

'Thank you so much,' mum replied.

Maureen walked us to the door and mum was still chatting to her when we went outside. I was feeling better about everything when suddenly I heard laughing. *Oh no! Kyla!*

Kyla and some other girls take a photo of Meghan. Meghan is very angry but she ignores them.

Kyla and a couple of other girls were standing on the other side of the road and ... they were taking another photo of me. I wanted to run over the road and tell Kyla to stop. I wanted to break her stupid phone! But I didn't want mum to know about the bullying so I just turned around and pretended[2] they weren't there.

'Come on, mum, let's go,' I said. 'Leah is waiting for us.'

'I'm coming, love,' mum shouted happily.

***Think***

**Why are volunteers special? Do you do any volunteer work?**

Kyla takes a photo of Meghan outside the food bank.

1 **chat** informal conversation
2 **pretended** behaved like the situation was different from the reality

FOOD BANK ALL WELCOME
#theyellowstickergirl
#totalcharitycase

## Reading Comprehension

**1 Read and answer the questions about Chapter 3. Use a maximum of 4 words.**

Where did Meghan want to go? *Home*

1 Who made Meghan feel better? ________

2 What did Leah paint? ________

3 What do Meghan's mum and dad have to pay?

________

4 Where do Meghan and her mum go for food?

________

5 Who helps Meghan and her mum at the food bank?

________

6 Who is with some other girls outside the food bank?

________

## Grammar

**2 Put the words in the correct order.**

wrote kids post Some the on comments horrible
*Some kids wrote horrible comments on the post.*

1 about bullies hasn't her told mum dad and Meghan the still

________

2 bill received parents gas Meghan's a have

________

3 greeted they Maureen arrived when Meghan at bank the and food mum her

________

4 her mum and never a to Meghan been bank before have food

________

5 saw Meghan food of lot tables a the on

________

6 better she again saw until Kyla felt Meghan

________

## Writing · A2 Key

**3 You're Meghan. Write an informal email to Maureen.**
**In your email:**

- Thank Maureen for her help last Saturday.
- Tell her Leah loved the chocolate milk.
- Ask about the opening times at the food bank next Saturday.

**Write between 25 and 35 words.**

*Before-reading Activity*

## Speaking

**4 Discuss these questions with a partner. Now read Chapter 4 and see if you were right.**

1. Will Kyla publish the photo of Meghan outside the food bank?
2. Will Meghan tell her mum and dad about the bullying?
3. Will Meghan and her mum go back to the food bank?
4. Will Meghan make any friends at the food bank?

## Chapter 4

# An Unexpected Ally

9 I wanted to be happy too but all the way home on the bus, I had a heavy heart. My phone pinged as soon as I got in the house. Tagged again. I thought about this week's hashtag … #foodbankgirl? #nomoney#nosupermarket?

Meghan is really sad. There are horrible comments on her phone.

I didn't want to look but I wanted to know what people were saying about me. *Be brave, Meghan! Ok, here goes.* I looked at my screen. There was another big photo of me and the hashtag #theyellowstickergirl#totalcharitycase. The worst thing was the comments though: 'Disappear, you sad loser!' and 'Tell your lazy[1] dad to get a job!' That was it, I couldn't read any more. I threw my phone on the floor and lay on my bed crying into my pillow. Why were people so horrible? My poor dad wasn't lazy, he was fantastic. After a few minutes, I heard a knock on my bedroom door. It was mum.

'Come and have a vanilla yoghurt, love,' she said as she came into my room but she stopped when she saw me on the bed.

'What's wrong, Meggie?' she asked. 'Come here, love.'

1 **lazy** a person who doesn't want to work or do anything

Mum gave me a big hug and I really wanted to tell her about Kyla and the other kids at school.

She wants to tell her mum about the bullying.

'Remember, you can tell me and dad anything Meggie,' mum continued.

'I know but you and dad have enough problems at the moment,' I said.

'Listen to me, Meggie,' mum said in her serious voice. 'Your dad and I have some money problems, that's all. The most important thing for us is that you and Leah are happy. Now, tell me what's wrong.'

Between my tears, I told mum everything. I told her about the photos at the supermarket, at the bus stop and outside the food bank. I told her about my new nickname, 'The Yellow Sticker Girl' and about how everyone laughed and pointed at me.

Mum listened quietly and then she finally said, 'Ok, don't worry about anything, Meghan. I'll go to school on Monday morning and talk to the headteacher.'

*No! No! No!*

'Mum, please don't go to school. Everyone will see you!'

Mum agreed not to go to school ...YET... but there were two conditions: I had to tell her

Meghan tells her mum all about the bullying. Her mum wants to go to school and talk to the headteacher but Meghan doesn't want her to. They agree that Meghan will tell her mum everything in the future and that she has to speak to her form teacher.

everything from now on and I had to speak to my form teacher[1] about the situation. *Great!*

Lucky for me, I got a bad cold that week and stayed home from school. TV in bed? Tick! No homework? Tick! No bullies? Tick. What a great week! By Saturday I was better and decided to go to the food bank with mum after work. I liked Maureen and I really wanted some more vanilla yoghurt. 😉 But my good luck was about to end ... as soon as we entered the hall, I saw Kyla! *What was she doing here?!* Mum saw her too and waved[2]. Kyla was with her mum and two little brothers and they all came over. *No! Please!* Kyla didn't look like her usual self though and she certainly wasn't laughing now.

Meghan has a cold and doesn't go to school all week. She sees Kyla and her family at the food bank on Saturday. Kyla's dad hasn't got a job. Meghan has to help Kyla.

'Is everything ok?' mum asked Kyla's mum.

'No, not really,' Kyla's mum replied sadly. 'My husband is unemployed[3] at the moment.'

'Don't worry,' mum said. 'We're in the same situation but everyone here is really friendly. Meghan, go and show Kyla what to do.'

*What? Me?*

I was about to protest but mum gave me one of THOSE looks. I knew I didn't have any choice. Kyla didn't look very happy either but I took her

Meghan helps Kyla at the food bank.

1 **form teacher** class coordinator
2 **waved** greeted with a hand movement
3 **unemployed** doesn't have a job

PASTA
RICE

over to a table where there was some rice and pasta in a box and gave her a shopping bag.

I thought mum was crazy! I didn't want to talk to my bully and I definitely didn't want to help her. I wanted to be mean[1] to Kyla. I wanted to make her feel embarrassed. I wanted to make her feel as bad as she made me feel at school. I wanted to ... I stopped and looked at Kyla. She looked so sad and scared.

Meghan wants to be horrible to Kyla but then she sees that she is sad and scared. Kyla says sorry to Meghan. Kyla's situation at home is terrible.

'Look, Kyla,' I said. 'It's not...'

Kyla interrupted me, 'No, Meghan, there's something I need to say first: I'm sorry.'

*Sorry? Wow! I wasn't expecting that!*

'You're sorry?' I asked.

'Yes,' replied Kyla. 'Really sorry.'

'Why did you do it?' I asked.

'I didn't want people to know that my dad hasn't got a job and that we haven't got any money,' she confessed. 'I didn't want people to laugh at me so I got them to laugh at you.'

*Great! I was a distraction[2]!*

I was still a bit mad but then Kyla started to tell me about her situation at home and it was terrible. Her mum was sick so she couldn't work and then her dad lost his job last year. They didn't

1 **mean** horrible
2 **distraction** something to take away the attention

have enough money to pay the rent[1] or bills and she was worried about her two little brothers.

I still didn't really understand why she bullied me but I understood how it felt to want to protect a brother or sister. Maybe me and Kyla had more in common than we thought. I decided to give her a chance[2].

'Look, let's start again, Kyla,' I suggested. 'We were friends at primary school, maybe we can be friends again.'

'Really? Thank you, Meghan,' she replied.

We were talking about all the fun we had in Miss Murphy's class at St. John Fisher Primary when Maureen interrupted us.

Meghan and Kyla talk about their old school.

'Girls!' she shouted. 'We have a small problem. Two of our volunteers are sick today and can't come in and help. Saturdays are our busiest day so I need two new volunteers.'

Kyla and I looked at each other.

'Do you mean...?' started Kyla.

'You want us to...?' I asked.

'Yes, yes. Come on girls,' replied Maureen. 'You are my two new volunteers. Remember: smile, bag, food and smile again.'

Maureen wants the girls to help at the food bank.

Kyla and I laughed and followed Maureen to one

1 **rent** money you pay to live in an apartment or house
2 **chance** possibility

of the tables. We passed mum on the way and she gave me a thumbs up. *Why are mums always right?!*

Lots of people visit the food bank. Some people need food but other people bring donations. Kyla and Meghan are happy about this.

Our first customer was Mrs Worthing, a sweet old lady. She lived on her own and didn't have any family. We tried to fill her bag with tinned goods but she only wanted a couple of things.

'Save the good stuff for the kiddies[1],' she said. 'I'm fine with a couple of tins of beans.'

There were lots of other people after Mrs Worthing. Some of them were new to the food bank and some of them were regulars. But not all the people who came that day needed food, some of them BROUGHT it. Mr Polonski from the mini-market brought some sandwiches and biscuits; Mrs Duffy from the greengrocer's brought some bananas and Mrs Singh from the chemist's brought some nappies[2] and shampoo. It wasn't only local business people who donated[3] things to the food bank; I saw a couple of families from my street coming in with parcels.

'Look,' I said to Kyla. 'There are so many people who want to help.'

'I know,' she replied. 'It's amazing, isn't it?'

I looked around the hall and suddenly felt happy and proud that I was helping too.

*Think*
**Why is it important to tell an adult about bullying?**

Meghan and Kyla become volunteers at the food bank.

1 **kiddies** small children
2 **nappies** something babies wear to absorb their urine and poop
3 **donated** gave things for free

SOUP

## Reading · A2 Key

**1 Complete the sentences about Chapter 4 with the correct answer (A, B or C ).**

Meghan *looked* at the photo on her screen.

**A** saw **B** looked **C** watched

1 She ________ a knock on her bedroom door.
**A** felt **B** touched **C** heard

2 Meghan's mum and dad have ________ money problems.
**A** a **B** some **C** any

3 Meghan agreed to tell her mum ________ from now on.
**A** everything **B** something **C** nothing

4 Meghan ________ Kyla at the food bank.
**A** met **B** found **C** see

5 Kyla apologised ________ Meghan.
**A** at **B** with **C** to

6 Some people ________ things to the foodbank.
**A** bought **B** brought **C** given

## Grammar

**2 Find and circle the mistakes in the sentences. Correct the sentences. One sentence is correct.**

The situation at school get will worse.

*The situation at school will get worse.*

1 Meghan's mum go to school won't on Monday.
2 Meghan going to is speak to her form teacher.
3 What this week's hashtag will be?
4 Meghan isn't going to talk to the headteacher.
5 Meghan's mum and help her will.
6 Kyla and Meghan are going to be friends again?

## Writing · A2 Key

21st Century Skills

**3 You're Kyla. Write a message to Meghan.**
**In your message:**

- Thank her for helping you at the food bank.
- Tell her you had fun volunteering.
- Invite her to your house on Friday.

**Write between 25 and 35 words.**

*Before-reading Activity*

## Reading · A2 Key

10 **4 Listen to the start of Chapter 5 and choose the correct answer (A, B or C).**

Meghan saw Kyla at *school* on Monday.

**A** home **B** school **C** the food bank

**1** Kyla's friends were ________ about the photos and comments.
**A** angry **B** excited **C** sorry

**2** Kyla and Meghan agree to talk to their ________ teacher about their problems and the bullying.
**A** physics **B** form **C** head

**3** They want their teacher to know that cyberbullying is a ________ problem.
**A** big **B** small **C** kids

**4** Meghan thinks that maybe the teacher could organise a ________ assembly.
**A** school **B** town **C** class

**5** Meghan wants to help people ________.
**A** more **B** les **C** the same

**6** Meghan wants to ask ________ for more bread and cake.
**A** Mr Turner **B** old people **C** neighbours

## *Chapter 5*

# Community Spirit

10 I saw Kyla at school on Monday. She was with her friends and I decided to just walk past but suddenly I heard my name.

'Meghan!' shouted Kyla. 'Come here a minute!'

I went over and suddenly her friends were all around me.

'Sorry about the photos, Meghan,' one of them said.

'And the horrible comments,' added another.

*Wow! More apologies*[1]*!*

Kyla's friends say sorry to Meghan at school. Kyla and Meghan agree to talk to their form teacher together about their problems. They want the teacher to talk to the class about bullying.

Kyla smiled at me and suggested that we talked to our form teacher together.

'We can tell him about our problems at home ... and the bullying,' she said sadly.

'OK,' I agreed. I didn't want Kyla to get in trouble but I did want our teacher to know that life was hard for a lot of kids and that cyberbullying[2] was a big problem. Maybe the teacher could organise a class assembly about being kind and helping others.

1 **apologies** when people say sorry
2 **cyberbullying** online bullying using photos, videos, messages or comments

*Hmmm. Helping others? What could I do to help other people more?*

I suddenly had an idea … I could ask Mr Turner for more bread and cake at the end of my Saturday shift and take it to the food bank. Or I could deliver it to some of the old people who lived near me and didn't have enough money for treats. I really liked the idea.

11 I thought about my ideas all week and decided to speak to Mr Turner on Saturday.

I told him all about my family's situation, about the food bank and about my idea for helping more people. He was happy to help.

**Meghan asks Mr Turner to donate bread and cakes to the food bank. He agrees.**

'That sounds like a great idea, Meghan,' he said. 'And you know I don't like food waste.'

I was so excited and I couldn't wait to tell Kyla.

'Kyla, listen to this,' I said as soon as I saw her.

I explained everything to Kyla and she was really enthusiastic.

'That's brilliant, Meghan,' she said. 'But maybe we can do more.'

*More? Wow! That sounded exciting!*

'Tell me, Kyla,' I said. 'What's your idea?"

'I want to use social media for something positive,' she said. 'I want to write a post about

Meghan and Kyla use social media to ask for food bank donations.

The food bank receives lots of donations. Meghan's dad gets a new job.

the food bank and ask people to make donations.'

*Genius!*

Kyla had a LOT of followers[1] and hundreds of people saw her post. The food bank received new donations every week from businesses and local people. I was really happy and then about a month later, things got even better. 'I've got a job, Meggie Moo!' dad shouted one evening.

Meghan and Kyla always go to the supermarket after 6:00 p.m. They buy yellow sticker items.

We had enough money now but I still worked at the bakery - I loved that job - and I still went to the food bank every Saturday with Kyla to help Maureen. After we finished, Kyla and I always went to the supermarket together, but never before 6:00 p.m.! We loved to look at all the stuff on offer[2] in the chiller cabinet on aisle 17. Sometimes we found some unusual yellow sticker ingredients for dinner.

'What's kale?' I asked.

'Looks like a kind of cabbage,' Kyla replied.

'Ok. It's only 45p. Maybe I can use it in a stir-fry[3] with these mushrooms and this beef,' I said.

'Sounds like a plan!' laughed Kyla.

1 **followers** people who read and like your social media posts
2 **on offer** with a lower price
3 **stir-fry** a Chinese dish where you cook meat / vegetables in a wok

❯ Meghan and Kyla use social media to ask for donations to the food bank.

DONATE TO YOUR LOCAL FOOD BANK!

Meghan and Kyla make some great dishes with their yellow sticker ingredients. They want to share their recipes and ideas about reducing food waste.

Kyla often slept over at my house on Saturday evenings and we spent hours inventing recipes with our yellow sticker ingredients. Ok, so maybe our fish and apple rice wasn't the best combination 😉 but our pasta bake with tuna, peppers, onions and cheese was delicious! It cost less than 2 pounds to make and everyone loved it!

'We make some really nice dishes,' Kyla said suddenly.

'I know,' I agreed. 'They taste great and they are really cheap too.'

'Plus we are reducing[1] food waste,' she added.

'We are!' I smiled. 'And we can freeze our leftovers[2] too, so there is zero waste!'

'We are just so cool!' she laughed. 'Seriously, we should share our ideas.'

'But how?' I asked.

'SOCIAL MEDIA!' we shouted in unison.

'We need our own page,' Kyla said. 'What can we call it?'

'We need something original,' I replied. 'How about The Yellow…?'

'Sticker Girls!' finished Kyla. 'I love it!'

'Me too,' I smiled.

They create their own social media page called 'The Yellow Sticker Girls'.

Meghan and Kyla invent their own yellow sticker recipes and start a social media page together.

*Think*

**How do Meghan and Kyla help to stop food waste?**

1 **reducing** making less
2 **leftovers** food you don't eat

The
YELLOW
STICKER
GIRLS

## Reading Comprehension

**1 Read and write True (T) or false (F) next to each sentence. Correct the false sentences.**

| | | T | F |
|---|---|---|---|
| | Kyla didn't say hello to Meghan at school on Monday. *Kyla did say hello to Meghan at school on Monday.* | ☐ | ☑ |
| 1 | Meghan suggested talking to the form teacher. | ☐ | ☐ |
| 2 | Meghan wanted to get Kyla into trouble. | ☐ | ☐ |
| 3 | Mr Turner was happy to help Meghan. | ☐ | ☐ |
| 4 | Kyla had the idea of using social media for something positive. | ☐ | ☐ |
| 5 | Meghan and Kyla didn't use their yellow sticker ingredients to invent new recipes. | ☐ | ☐ |
| 6 | Meghan and Kyla called their social media page 'The Yellow Sticker Girls'. | ☐ | ☐ |

## Speaking and Writing

21st Century Skills

**2A Were you surprised that Kyla and Meghan became good friends? Do you like their idea of using social media to stop food waste? Why? / Why not?**

**2B How could you use social media for a good cause in your community? Talk to your partner and write your ideas.**

## Vocabulary

**3 How many key words can you remember from *The Yellow Sticker Girl*?**
**Read the clues and complete the crossword.**

Down

1 Something you write on social media (n) or publish. (v)

2 Someone who lives in your street. (n)

3 On the internet. (n)

4 It's not your real name. (n)

5 A symbol you put before or after a social media post. (n)

Across

1 Opinions you write about photos/ posts on the internet. (n)

2 A person who is unkind to someone in a weaker position. (n)

3 Very hungry. (adj)

4 Something you don't use (n) or maximise. (v)

5 Decrease, lower. (v)

*Focus on...*

# Food Waste

At the start of the story, Meghan is hungry but there is no food in the fridge. Meghan's parents don't have enough money to buy food. Food poverty is a growing problem and means that it is more important now than ever before to stop food waste.

## What is industry food waste?

Food waste can occur when the food that farmers grow and manufacturers produce is not sold. It is important for food suppliers to meet market demand; they must produce the right amount of food. When there is too much food on the market, it goes to waste; when there is too little food on the market, prices increase, poor people go hungry and the food goes to waste.

## What is domestic food waste?

Shoppers often buy more food than they need from the supermarket. Some people like having a full fridge, *just in case*, and other people cannot resist the supermarket promotions like buy 2, get 1 free. It is often cheaper to buy big packets of food rather than single portions but the reality is that people often throw that extra food in the bin and it becomes food waste.

# The United Nation's Mission

The United Nations wants to reduce food waste by 2030.
Currently around 1.3 billion tonnes of food are wasted each year, that's approximately 1/3 of all food produced for the global market.

Goal 12 on the UN's Agenda for Sustainable Development published in 2015, promotes 'responsible consumption and production'. To achieve this goal, politicians, business leaders and individuals must work together for change.

# Initiatives Against Food Waste

Supermarkets in the UK usually discount unsold fresh food, especially at the end of the day. Yellow stickers often indicate a reduced price. Some supermarkets have also taken 'best before' dates off fresh food. This means that food is not automatically discounted or thrown away; retailers and consumers can check the products themselves. Restaurants are also doing more: they donate leftover food to charity, sell it on an app or send it to a recycling plant.

## Task – Social Media

**Write a post about food waste.**
**Include:**

- why we need to stop food waste;
- what we can all do to make a difference.

**REMEMBER:** *When you waste food, you waste energy too and this has an impact on climate change. Save food, save the planet!*

*Focus on...*

# Bullying

Many famous people were bullied at school or online, just like Meghan, but they now have happy and successful lives. Let's take a look at some of their stories.

## Justin Timberlake

This American singer-songwriter and actor was bullied at school. His classmates thought he was weird and called him horrible names. Timberlake's mum taught him that it was good to be different because it is people who are different who can make a difference in the world. In fact, his performances have impacted fans around the world and he has won numerous awards including ten Grammys.

***Are you or anyone you know being bullied?***
*Speak to a responsible adult and remember, things will get better.*

## Kate Middleton

Catherine Elizabeth Middleton was miserable at school. There was a group of mean girls who always laughed at her because she was tall and thin. Now she is a princess and a style icon who represents the British royal family at important events. She hasn't forgotten what it feels like to be a victim of bullying though; guests to her wedding with Prince William were asked to make donations to the Beatbullying charity.

## Tom Daley

This British Olympic diver was targeted by bullies at school. He was different because he was already an accomplished athlete and because his dad had brain cancer. The bullying was so bad that Daley had to move schools after he competed in the Beijing Olympics in 2008. Daley was only 14 years old when he competed for the first time at Olympic level and his dad died when he was 17 years old. He is now one of the best divers in the world: he won an Olympic gold medal at the Olympic Games in Tokyo in 2022.

## Millie Bobbie Brown

This American actress was only 11 years old when she became an international star. As the protagonist in *Stranger Things*, a major Netflix show, she received a lot of attention from the media and the public. The hate comments on social media made Brown insecure but she talked to her family and friends and they helped her. The young actress doesn't manage her social media accounts now and is focused on her own personal development.

## What can we learn from these celebrity stories?

We can learn that it's good to be different; that it doesn't matter what other people think; that we can change our lives; that good things can happen after bad things and that it always helps to talk to family and friends.

### Task

**Imagine a friend is being bullied.**

- What should / shouldn't they do?
- Write down your advice.

## *Test Yourself*

**How much can you remember? Choose A, B or C to complete the sentences about the story.**

At the beginning of the story Meghan is

**A** thirsty. ~~**B**~~ hungry. **C** tired.

**1** Meghan and her dad arrive at the supermarket

**A** before 18:00. **B** at 18:00. **C** after 18:00.

**2** A shop assistant puts yellow stickers on the food to

**A** reduce the price. **B** increase the price. **C** halve the price.

**3** Kyla gives Meghan a horrible

**A** photo. **B** nickname. **C** gift.

**4** Meghan gets a Saturday job in a

**A** bakery. **B** clothes shop. **C** supermarket.

**5** The kids at school laugh at Meghan and she hides in the

**A** canteen. **B** classroom. **C** toilets.

**6** Meghan and her mum go to get food from a

**A** food bank. **B** supermarket. **C** market.

**7** Meghan's mum says Meghan has to speak to her

**A** headteacher. **B** form teacher. **C** dad.

**8** Meghan and Kyla become Maureen's new

**A** students. **B** shop assistants. **C** volunteers.

**9** Mr Turner is happy to help Meghan because he doesn't like

**A** food waste. **B** bread. **C** cake.

## *Syllabus*

**Topics**
Family
Friendship
Food poverty
Food waste
Gender equality
Online bullying

**Verbs**
Positive and negative imperative forms
Present simple
Present continuous
Past simple (regular and irregular forms)
Past continuous
Present perfect simple
Future with *going to* and *will*
Modals (*can, could, have to, need to*)
Common phrasal verbs

**Adjectives**
Absolute forms
Comparative and superlative forms

**Adverbs**
Regular and irregular forms

# Teen ELi Readers

### *Stage 1*
Maureen Simpson, *In Search of a Missing Friend*
Charles Dickens, *Oliver Twist*
Geoffrey Chaucer, *The Canterbury Tales*
Janet Borsbey & Ruth Swan, *The Boat Race Mystery*
Lucy Maud Montgomery, *Anne of Green Gables*
Mark Twain, *A Connecticut Yankee in King Arthur's Court*
Mark Twain, *The Adventures of Huckleberry Finn*
Angela Tomkinson, *Great Friends!*
Edith Nesbit, *The Railway Children*
Eleanor H. Porter, *Pollyanna*
Anna Sewell, *Black Beauty*
Kenneth Grahame, *The Wind in the Willows*

### *Stage 2*
Elizabeth Ferretti, *Dear Diary...*
Angela Tomkinson, *Loving London*
Mark Twain, *The Adventures of Tom Sawyer*
Mary Flagan, *The Egyptian Souvenir*
Maria Luisa Banfi, *A Faraway World*
Frances Hodgson Burnett, *The Secret Garden*
Robert Louis Stevenson, *Treasure Island*
Elizabeth Ferretti, *Adventure at Haydon Point*
William Shakespeare, *The Tempest*
Angela Tomkinson, *Enjoy New York*
Frances Hodgson Burnett, *Little Lord Fauntleroy*
Michael Lacey Freeman, *Egghead*
Michael Lacey Freeman, *Dot to Dot*
Silvana Sardi, *The Boy with the Red Balloon*
Silvana Sardi, *Scotland is Magic!*
Silvana Sardi, *Garpur: My Iceland*
Silvana Sardi, *Follow your Dreams*
Gabriele Rebagliati, *Naoko: My Japan*
Sarah Gudgeon, *The Yellow Sticker Girl*

### *Stage 3*
Anna Claudia Ramos, *Expedition Brazil*
Charles Dickens, *David Copperfield*
Mary Flagan, *Val's Diary*
Maureen Simpson, *Destination Karminia*
Anonymous, *Robin Hood*
Jack London, *The Call of the Wild*
Louisa May Alcott, *Little Women*
Gordon Gamlin, *Allan: My Vancouver*